PALEO DIET FOR WEIGHT LOSS

EAT WELL AND GET HEALTHY

100 EASY RECIPES FOR BEGINNERS

gluten-free
sugar-free
legume-free
dairy-free

Claudia Grosser
Susan Risse

TABLE OF CONTENTS

INTRODUCTION

This Paleo diet consists of trying to return to our beginnings and develop a diet that is based on those foods that cave dwellers used to eat ages ago. To lose weight, get healthier and be wholly transformed, scientists recommend imitating our ancestor's diet. This means that your diet should mainly consist of fish and meat dishes, a considerable amount of fruits and vegetables in fresh form, in addition to mushrooms, seeds, and nuts. In reasonable quantities, it is permissible to consume vegetable oils. It is recommended to eliminate legumes, cereals, dairy products, fatty meats, vegetables rich in carbohydrates, and food with high salt content, like convenience foods and salted nuts because salt has a negative effect on kidneys and leads to pain in the joints.

These people, who had almost no cooking skills and limited knowledge about their health, survived in various environments. Even without the advanced medical knowledge that we have now, these people were able to thrive in that wild environment.

Things have changed since then, but Paleo has made a resurgence into the mainstream. This particular diet wants people to return to the ancient ways of eating. The point is to eat food with as little processing as possible. The diets from pre-historic times provided all the nutrients that we needed and lacked many of the extra sugars that have been added by modern processing of foods.

Paleo diet is based explicitly on the idea of hunting and gathering. Foods like vegetables, fruits, nuts, seeds, meat, and fish are allowed in this diet.

Paleo diet ensures that even when you're burning the fat in your body, you can still have enough energy to do everything that your day demands of you. Paleo takes into account everything that your body needs to thrive, such as having stable blood sugar and a proper metabolism.

Without going further let's go over the main benefits of the paleo diet. Paleo diet has the following benefits:

It improves overall hormonal background.

It helps build muscle mass. The growth of muscle mass is due to the regular consumption of low-fat meat, which contains a sufficient number of natural proteins.

The followers of this diet are virtually not suffering from depression and have an increased stress resistance.

Reduces the risk of cardiovascular diseases. Decreased levels of blood cholesterol significantly reduce the risk of developing diseases of the central organ of the circulatory system.

Paleo diet is an excellent way to prevent atherosclerosis.

Normalizes blood pressure.

The skin will improve, the hair will become more healthy and shiny.

Paleo doesn't cut out everything. The diet focuses on getting your body nutrient-rich foods. A meal made up of fruits and vegetables with a portion of meat or seafood with some oil can improve your health.

While this doesn't sound like it will work for weight loss, it does. All the food you consume right now is either used for energy or turned into fat. To lose fat that is already in your body, you'll want to ensure that your body is not creating additional fat.

There's no way around eating carbs. The best that you can do with your diet is to measure how many carbs you take and ensure the carbs you are consuming are high-quality, nutrient-dense complex carbohydrates. When you've cut out as many bad carbs as possible, you'll find that your body will turn to the fat stores and chip away at those, converting them into extra energy.

Weight loss with Paleo isn't about putting your body through hell. Your diet will work with your body and provide all the nutrients you need for a delicious meal. It may be the most enjoyable way that you have ever lost weight.

What are you waiting for?

Join the big community of people all over the world who already decided to start a Paleo diet for healthier and happier life.

Principles and Rules of Paleo Diet

Several basic rules and principles should be followed to achieve a final positive result with the paleo diet.

- The most important rule is to eat the food that was available to distant ancestors. Adherents of the diet recommend to make a preliminary menu for the week and take into account that the number of meat dishes should not exceed vegetable. Hunting for primitive people was not always successful, and the meat was not present every day in their diet.

- During the Paleo diet, there is no need to eat food strictly portioned at the same time. Also, do not control the number of fats and carbohydrates that are contained in foods. The main rule is the use of products that are allowed for the consumption as part of the diet. However, even if you break the menu, you do not have to go through an individual phase anew.

- The key to success is the use of exclusively natural products, such as roots, berries, plants, herbs, fruits, and vegetables from organic farms. The products used should not contain pesticides and preservatives. It is likely that additional costs will accompany this, but this requirement is essential for achieving the desired results.

- In ancient times people used uncooked fruits and vegetables for eating, and meat – cooked on the fire. When observing the paleo diet, it is recommended to follow this principle, though you can use a more complicated way of preparing dishes. Paleo adherents believe that the main thing is the right ingredients, and how the meal is ready and how it is served does not matter.

- Do not forget about the level of physical activity. Lead an active lifestyle because our ancestors worked "hard and fast" to get their food and survive. A simple morning run or a free exercise is also an integral part of achieving the desired result with the paleo diet.

- As for the intervals between meals, eat if there is an actual feeling of hunger (and not for the company, out of sadness, or because you have not eaten for a long time), but not less than three times a day. The amounts of servings are not limited, but one must remember that a reasonable person has common sense and sense of proportion. Try to eat less and move more, if possible.

- Do not eat carbohydrates in large quantities and simple carbs (sugar, sweet soda, fast food, confectionery sweets, and convenience foods) should be wholly excluded from the diet. Since the carbohydrate diet is contrary to the human genome, which has not changed even despite the long and tortuous evolutionary process.

- Entirely exclude from your diet industrial sugar (natural honey can still be consumed). Sugar not only provokes the development of acute diseases but also contributes to obesity and increases the frequency and intensity of insulin releases into the blood.

- Any meat used in the paleo diet must be dietary, low-fat. Obviously, you'll need to avoid exceedingly handled meats and meats that are high in fat (spam, wieners, *etc.*).

What to Eat on Paleo Diet

The list of products you can eat on the paleo diet is very extensive. Here it is:

- Meat: poultry, pork, veal, beef, lamb, bacon, rabbit, venison. The strictest followers use the only meat of wild animals, birds or organic meat obtained by growing animals without the use of supplements.
- Seafood and fish caught in the seas, oceans, rivers.
- Eggs of quails, ostriches, chickens, grown naturally.
- Vegetables: asparagus, zucchini, cabbage, cauliflower, broccoli, carrots, artichokes, spinach, celery, green onions, *etc.* grown without the use of fertilizers.
- Fruits: bananas, avocados, apricots, grapes, kiwi, lime, lemons, oranges, tangerines, pears, watermelon, melon, figs, mango, pineapple, passion fruit and papaya, *etc.* grown without the use of fertilizers.
- Berries: blueberries, blackberries, cranberries, cherries, raspberries, strawberries, *etc.* grown without the use of fertilizers.
- Allowed fats: walnut oil, linseed oil, olive oil, avocado oil, macadamia nut oil and coconut oil (only in small amounts).
- Mushrooms.
- Sea salt, natural seasonings, and spices.
- Apple cider vinegar and soy sauce (naturally fermented without addition of wheat).
- Nuts: hazelnuts, cashews, almonds, pine nuts, pecans, cashews, walnuts, pumpkin seeds and sunflower seeds, except for peanuts, as they are a representative of legumes.
- Water, infusions of herbs, coconut milk are allowed for drinks. Some include coffee and alcohol in small amounts.

- Despite the fact that in the Paleo Age gelatin was not present, the paleo adepts use it for cooking.

One thing you should know about meat

Specialists evaluate that our precursors expended a balanced proportion of calories from meats to deliver. Since you need to eat a great deal of serving of mixed greens to drink a similar measure of calories in a steak, the paleo eating regimen ought to in a perfect world incorporate most products of the soil. Be that as it may, many individuals don't understand that and indulge meat. Expending overabundance protein and insufficient carbs can cause kidney harm and furthermore increment your danger of osteoporosis. Besides, since a large portion of the present chickens are higher in immersed fat than those of yesteryear, it can build the danger of coronary illness.

About Nuts

We adore nuts, and they are unequivocally paleo abstain from food benevolent. Be cautious however, as cashews are high in fat and, for reasons unknown, it's unfathomably simple to eat a whole container of them in one sitting. In case you are attempting to get in shape, confine the quantity of nuts you are devouring.

About Fruits

Fruits are heavenly, as well as awesome for you. Natural products contain critical measures of fructose which is still sugar. If you want to lose weight using the paleo diet, you will have to concentrate on vegetables and eat fewer fruits.

About Alcohol

Alcohol is not part of the paleo diet, but red wine can be an option to a paleo drink.

14

What Not to Eat on Paleo Diet

The following products are not allowed in the paleo diet:

- All cereals without exception: grains, bread, flour, and pasta. Most grains contain gluten, which contributes to the destruction of the intestinal flora, provokes the emergence of bacterial infections, and inhibits the absorption of vitamins. A specific group of lectins, contained in cereals and legumes, reduces intestinal absorbency and weakens the immune system.

- Legumes: peas, peanuts, beans, lentils, soybeans contain lectin and phytates, which slow down digestion or even wholly remove such useful elements from the body as iron, calcium, magnesium, zinc.

- In the original version of Paleo diet, there is no place for milk and dairy products. The human body is ill-adapted to absorb the milk, which is why lactose and casein intolerance is so often experienced. Coconut milk, nuts and cabbage can be considered as a source of calcium.

- Sugar, artificial sweeteners and the whole group of products with their content.

- The list of prohibited products also includes potatoes. Fans of this root can replace it with sweet potato.

7-day Paleo diet meal plan

Day 1:

Breakfast – Spinach Omelet

Lunch – Special Paleo Pork Chops with Sweet Apple Coleslaw

Snack – Berries or apple

Dinner – Delicious Paleo Salad

Day 2:

Breakfast – Tasty Apple Almond Coconut Medley

Lunch – Pesto Chicken

Snack – Banana

Dinner – Roasted Bell Pepper Soup

Day 3:

Breakfast – Ultimate Granola

Lunch – Beef Stew

Snack – Orange or grapefruit

Dinner – Chicken Eastern Surprise

Day 4:

Breakfast – Zucchini Casserole

Lunch – Kale Orange Chicken

Snack – Apple Cobbler

Dinner – Pumpkin Carrot Soup

Day 5:

Breakfast – Coconut Porridge

Lunch – Paleo Beef Stir Fry

Snack – Berries or banana

Dinner – Mint Zucchini Pasta With Pistachio Crumble

Day 6:

Breakfast – Paleo Pumpkin Pancakes

Lunch – Tahini Paste And Avocado Soup

Snack – Apple

Dinner – Chicken Salad

Day 7:

Breakfast – Paleo Breakfast Cookies

Lunch – Amazing Beef Lasagna

Snack – Chocolate Covered Figs

Dinner – Advanced Avocado Tuna Salad

Shopping list

Oils, Sauces and Staples
Coconut Oil
Apple cider vinegar
Extra-virgin olive oil
Sesame oil
Balsamic vinegar
Almond butter
Tahini paste
Ghee

Meat, Fish and Poultry
Beef steaks
Ground beef
Pork chops
Chicken fillets
Tuna
Bacon strips

Nuts and Seeds
Almonds
Cashews
Raw pine nuts
Raw pumpkin seeds
Raw sunflower seeds
Flax seeds
Sesame seeds
Unsalted pistachios
Walnuts
Pecans

Herbs and Spices
Salt (low sodium salt)
Sea Salt
Black pepper
Chili pepper (or chili flakes)
Cayenne pepper
Paprika
Baking soda (baking powder)
Basil leaves
Parsley
Cilantro
Sage springs
Mint leaves
Oregano (dried)
Coriander seeds
Pumpkin Pie spice
Cumin seeds (or cumin powder)
Cinnamon
Vanilla (vanilla extract)
Nutmeg
Turmeric

Eggs

Vegetables

Baby spinach
Spinach leaves
Kale
Lettuce
Arugula
Baby bok choy
White cabbage
Asparagus spears
Tomatoes
Cucumber
Radishes
Celery stalk
Fennel bulb
Red onions
Yellow onions
Shallot
Green onions (or scallions)
Garlic
Ginger
Chili pepper
Red bell peppers
Zucchini
Eggplant
Pumpkin
Carrots
Canned chopped tomatoes

Mushrooms

Fruits

Apples
Bananas
Avocados
Limes
Lemons
Oranges
Grapefruit
Berries
Strawberries
Dates
Figs

Extras

Mustard
Organic shredded coconut, unsweetened
Coconut milk
Coconut flour
Coconut aminos (coconut amino)
Coconut cream
Flaxseed golden meal
Almond flour
Almond milk
Raw honey
Pure maple syrup
Raisins
Dark chocolate

Paleo Breakfasts

Zucchini Casserole

Ingredients:

- 5 eggs
- Mushrooms, ½ cup, sliced
- ½ red onion, chopped
- Pepper and salt to taste
- 3 large zucchini

Directions:

1. Season beaten eggs with pepper and salt. Mix all ingredients in a bowl alongside grated zucchini.
2. Add mixture to the pan coated with olive oil and cook for 6 minutes.
3. Prepare oven at 375 F
4. Bake the mixture for 14 more minutes; let it cool for a while and serve.

Servings: 4
Preparation time: 15 min
Cooking time: 20 min

Ultimate Granola

Ingredients:

- Coconut milk, 1 cup
- Fresh berries, 2 tablespoon
- Raw pumpkin seeds, 1 teaspoon
- Raw sunflower seeds, 1 teaspoon
- Raw pine nuts, 1 teaspoon

- Unsalted pistachios, 1 teaspoon
- Slivered almonds, 1 teaspoon
- Walnut pieces, 1 teaspoon
- Pecan pieces, 1 teaspoon

Directions:
1. Combine all nuts as well as seeds in a bowl.
2. Add berries to milk and set aside for a while until releases color and enjoy.

Servings: 1
Preparation time: 5 min
Cooking time: 15 min

Spinach Omelet

Ingredients:
- Minced chicken, 2 ounces
- Handful of baby spinach, chopped
- Pepper and salt to taste
- 2 beaten eggs
- Coconut oil for frying, 1 tablespoon
- Cayenne pepper to taste

Directions:
1. Cook chicken in pan coated with coconut oil until brown.
2. Season with salt as well as pepper.
3. Mix cayenne pepper, eggs as well as spinach, transfer to skillet and cook for 2-4 minutes before you serve.

Servings: 1
Preparation time: 10 min
Cooking time: 25 min

Tasty Apple Almond Coconut Medley

Ingredients:
- 1 pinch of salt
- Generous dose of cinnamon
- Handful of unsweetened coconut
- Handful of sliced almonds
- One-half apple cored and roughly diced
- Coconut milk

Directions:
Pulse all ingredients in a mixer and serve.

Servings: 1
Preparation time: 5 min
Cooking time: 10 min

Coconut Porridge

Ingredients:
- Flaxseed golden meal, 1 tablespoon
- Almond flour, 2 tablespoon
- Vanilla, 1 tablespoon
- A pinch of salt
- Organic shredded coconut, ¼ cup, unsweetened
- Coconut milk, 2/3 cup
- Honey to taste

22

- Slivered almonds, 1 tablespoon

Directions:
1. Add all ingredients except honey and almonds to the pan coated with coconut milk and cook on low heat.
2. Serve with topped almonds and honey.

Servings: 1
Preparation time: 5 min
Cooking time: 15 min

Paleo Pumpkin Pancakes

Ingredients:
- Pure maple syrup, ¼ cup
- Sea salt, ½ teaspoon
- Baking soda, ½ teaspoon
- Pumpkin pie spice, 1 teaspoon
- Flax seeds, ½ cup
- Almond flour, 2 cups
- Cinnamon, 1 teaspoon
- Vinegar, 1 teaspoon
- Almond milk, ½ cup
- Coconut oil, 2 tablespoon
- 4 eggs
- Pumpkin puree, 1 cup

Directions:
1. Mix wet and dry ingredients in two separate bowls.
2. Slowly transfer mixtures to one bowl and mix.

3. Make pancakes with mixture and fry until brown on both sides before serving.

Servings: 4
Preparation time: 10 min
Cooking time: 25 min

Paleo Breakfast Cookies

Ingredients:

- Chopped raisins, 2 tablespoons
- Chopped pecans, 2 tablespoons
- Diced strawberries, 2 tablespoons
- Baking powder, ½ teaspoon
- Sea salt, ¼ teaspoon
- Vanilla, ½ teaspoon
- Nutmeg, 1 teaspoon
- Cinnamon, ½ teaspoon
- 2 medium eggs lightly beaten
- 2 bananas, mashed
- Unsweetened shredded coconut, ½ cup
- 6 whole dates soaked and pitted in hot water
- Almond butter, ½ cup
- Coconut flour, ¼ cup

Directions:

1. Pulse dates in a mixer for one minute, add bananas, almond butter as well as coconut flour and pulse until well blended.

2. Add cinnamon, salt, eggs, vanilla, nutmeg, shredded coconut as well as baking powder and pulse for one more minute.
3. Fill dough with raisins, strawberries as well as pecans.
4. Cover the cookie sheet with parchment paper.
5. Form balls and flatten each one with your hands.
6. Bake cookies for 14 minutes on 350 F until brown and serve.

Servings: 4
Preparation time: 20 min
Cooking time: 30 min

Eggs, Mushrooms And Onion Bonanza

Ingredients:
- 4 hard boiled eggs, peeled and finely chopped
- 6 medium white mushrooms, finely chopped
- Coconut oil, 2 tablespoons
- Ground black pepper to taste
- 1 medium onion, finely diced

Directions:
1. Fry onions in a pan coated with coconut oil until brown.
2. Add mushrooms, fry for 5 more minutes and spoon frequently.
3. Let it cool for a while; serve with mixed eggs and pepper.

Servings: 2
Preparation time: 20 min
Cooking time: 15 min

Delish Veggie Hash With Eggs

Ingredients:

- 4 eggs, cooked
- Fresh spinach, 1 cup, chopped
- Cherry tomatoes, 1 cup, halved
- Pepper and salt to taste
- Mushroom, ½ cup, sliced
- Yellow squash, 1 cup, chopped
- Extra virgin olive oil, 2 tablespoons
- 2 cloves garlic, minced
- Sweet white onion, ¼ cup, chopped

Directions:

1. Fry onions for 3 minutes in a pan coated with olive oil; add squash and cook for 90 more seconds.
2. After adding mushrooms cook for 5 additional minutes.
3. Season with pepper and salt; add spinach as well as tomatoes until wilted and serve with cooked eggs.

Servings: 2
Preparation time: 15 min
Cooking time: 20 min

Outstanding Veggie Omelet

Ingredients:

- 3 scallions, sliced diagonal
- 1 carrot, matchstick cut
- 3 eggs, beaten
- 1 handful tiny broccoli

26

- Salt to taste
- Olive oil

Directions:
1. Fry broccoli florets as well as carrots in a pan coated with oil for 2 minutes.
2. Afterwards add scallions as well as eggs and serve with seasoned salt.

Servings: 2
Preparation time: 10 min
Cooking time: 15 min

Spicy Indian Omelet

Ingredients:
- Coconut grated, ¼ cup
- 4 green chili peppers, seeded and cut into strips
- Oil for cooking
- 1 onion, chopped
- 4 eggs, beaten
- Salt to taste

Directions:
1. Combine and mix chopped onion, green chili peppers, salt, beaten eggs as well as grated coconuts in a bowl.
2. Add it to the pan coated with oil and cook properly on both sides before serving.

Servings: 2
Preparation time: 10 min
Cooking time: 15 min

Basil And Walnut Eggs Divine

Ingredients:
- Walnuts, 1/3 cup, chopped
- 3 eggs
- Pepper and salt to taste
- Fresh basil, ½ cup, chopped
- Oil for cooking

Directions:
1. Cook eggs in a pan; add basil and cook for 1 more minute.
2. Season with salt as well as pepper and serve with heated walnuts.

Servings: 1
Preparation time: 10 min
Cooking time: 15 min

Divine Protein Muesli

Ingredients:
- Hemp protein, 1 tablespoon
- Unsweetened almond milk, 1 cup
- Cinnamon, ½ teaspoon
- Chocolate chips, 1 tablespoon
- Raisins, 1 tablespoon
- Raw almonds, 1 tablespoon
- Chopped walnuts, 1 tablespoon
- Coconut flakes, 1 cup, unsweetened

Directions:

1. Layer almonds, walnuts, raisins, chocolate chips as well as coconut flakes to a bowl.
2. Serve with splashed cinnamon, hemp protein as well as milk onto it.

Servings: 1
Preparation time: 5 min
Cooking time: 5 min

Spiced Granola

Ingredients:

- Hemp seeds, ¼ cups
- Coconut flakes, ½ cup
- Walnuts, ½ cup
- Salt to taste
- Vanilla extract, 2 teaspoons
- Nutmeg, 2 teaspoons
- Cinnamon, 2 teaspoons
- Coconut oil, 1/3 cup
- Almond flour, 1 ½ cups

Directions:

1. Prepare oven at 275 F.
2. Combine all ingredients in a bowl and scatter onto baking sheet.
3. Bake for 45 minutes and serve.

Servings: 4
Preparation time: 5 min
Cooking time: 45 min

Eggplant With Eggs

Ingredients:
- 3 medium eggs
- Pepper and salt to taste
- Coconut oil for frying
- 2 eggplants, sliced into discs

Directions:
1. Beat eggs and season with pepper and salt.
2. Dip discs in beaten eggs; add the discs to the pan coated with oil and prepare until brown on both sides before serving.

Servings: 2
Preparation time: 10 min
Cooking time: 25 min

Paleo Breakfast Stir Fry Recipe

Ingredients:
- Minced garlic, 1 teaspoon
- Spinach, 4 cups
- Leeks, 1 cup, chopped
- Chopped carrot, ½ cup
- Coconut oil, 1 teaspoon
- 4 eggs

Directions:
1. Season eggs with pepper and salt; add it to the pan coated with oil and transfer to a platter after making omelet.

2. Cook leeks, garlic as well as carrot in different skillet, add spinach and cook for one minute.
3. Serve scattered mixture onto omelet.

Servings: 4
Preparation time: 10 min
Cooking time: 25 min

Post-Workout Paleo Breakfast Bake

Ingredients:
- 6 eggs
- Dried thyme, ½ teaspoon
- Garlic powder, ½ teaspoon
- Paprika, ½ teaspoon
- Salt and pepper to taste
- 3 roughly chopped onions
- 4 sliced mushrooms
- Crumbled leftover Turkey patties, ¼ pound

Directions:
1. Prepare oven at 350 F.
2. Mix all ingredients and transfer it to baking sheet, bake for 45 minutes and serve.

Servings: 2
Preparation time: 10 min
Cooking time: 45 min

Silver Dollar Pancakes

Ingredients:
- 3 large eggs
- Water, 1 tablespoon
- Vanilla extract, 1 tablespoon
- Honey, 2 tablespoons
- Almond flour, 1 ½ cups
- Baking powder, ¼ teaspoon
- Coconut oil for cooking
- Sea salt, ¼ teaspoon

Directions:
1. Pulse eggs, vanilla, water as well as honey in a mixer; add baking powder, almond flour as well as salt and mix thoroughly.
2. Make pancakes with mixture and cook for 4 minutes before you serve.

Servings: 4
Preparation time: 10 min
Cooking time: 20 min

Soups

Tahini Paste And Avocado Soup

Ingredients:

- Spinach leaves, 1 cup
- 2 ripe avocados, peeled
- Tahini paste, 4 tablespoons
- 1 cucumber
- Water, 1 cup
- 1 garlic clove
- 1 lemon, juiced
- Pepper and salt to taste
- Chopped cilantro, 2 tablespoons

Directions:

1. Pulse all ingredients except cilantro in a mixer; process until smooth or for 2 minutes.
2. Serve with splashed cilantro.

Servings: 2
Preparation time: 10 min
Cooking time: 10 min

Pumpkin Carrot Soup

Ingredients:

- Pumpkin cubes, 2 cups
- Carrot juice, 1 cup
- Water, 1 cup
- Lemon juice, 2 tablespoons
- 1 Garlic clove

- 1 small sweet onion
- Turmeric, ½ teaspoon
- 1 pinch nutmeg
- Extra virgin olive oil, 2 tablespoons
- Sesame oil, ½ teaspoon
- Pepper and salt to taste
- Pumpkin seeds, 4 tablespoons

Directions:
1. Pulse all ingredients except pumpkin seeds.
2. Serve with splashed pumpkin seeds.

Servings: 2
Preparation time: 10 min
Cooking time: 10 min

Cashew And Tomato Soup

Ingredients:
- 4 ripe tomatoes
- ½ celery stalk
- Cashew nuts, ½ cup, soaked overnight
- 1 shallot
- 2 garlic cloves
- Water, 1 cup
- ½ lemon, juiced
- Pepper and salt to taste
- Olive oil, 2 tablespoons
- Chopped cilantro, 2 tablespoons

Directions:
Pulse salt, pepper, lemon juice, garlic, water, cashews, celery as well as tomato in a mixer; blend until creamy and serve with splashed cilantro.

Servings: 2
Preparation time: 10 min
Cooking time: 10 min

Spinach And Green Onion Soup

Ingredients:
- Spinach leaves, 4 cups
- 1 garlic clove
- 2 green onions
- 1 pinch nutmeg
- Cashew nuts, 1 cup, soaked overnight
- Water, 1 cup
- Lemon juice, 2 tablespoons
- Lemon zest, 1 tablespoon
- Pepper and salt to taste
- Olive oil, 2 tablespoons

Directions:
Pulse all the ingredients; process until creamy and serve in bowls.

Servings: 2
Preparation time: 5 min
Cooking time: 10 min

Roasted Bell Pepper Soup

Ingredients:

- 4 roasted bell peppers
- 2 large ripe tomatoes
- ½ fennel bulb
- 4 basil leaves
- ½ red onion
- ½ lemon, juiced
- Water, 1 cup
- ½ chili pepper, seeded
- 2 garlic cloves
- Pepper and salt to taste
- Extra virgin olive oil, 2 tablespoons

Directions:

Pulse chili, garlic, onion, basil, fennel, bell peppers, tomatoes, lemon juice as well as water in a mixer for 3 minutes; transfer to a bowl and serve with splashed olive oil.

Servings: 2
Preparation time: 40 min
Cooking time: 10 min

Zucchini And Pistachio Cold Soup

Ingredients:

- 3 young zucchinis, cubed
- 1 celery stalk
- Pistachio, ½ cup
- 1 avocado, peeled

- Lemon juice, 1 tablespoon
- Fresh thyme, 1 teaspoon
- Turmeric, ½ teaspoon
- 1 garlic clove
- Chopped onion, 1 tablespoon
- Pepper and salt to taste

Directions:
Pulse all ingredients in a mixer, process until smooth, flavor with salt as well as pepper. Serve.

Servings: 2
Preparation time: 15 min
Cooking time: 10 min

Lettuce And Cucumber Soup

Ingredients:
- ½ head lettuce, well rinsed and shredded
- 1 large cucumber
- 1 ripe avocado, peeled
- 1 garlic clove
- Lemon juice, 1 tablespoon
- Water, 1 cup
- Coconut cream, ½ cup
- Pepper and salt to taste
- Dried oregano, ½ teaspoon

Directions:
Pulse all ingredients in a mixer; blend until creamy and serve.

Servings: 2
Preparation time: 10 min
Cooking time: 10 min

Beet Creamy Soup

Ingredients:

- 2 raw beets, peeled and cubed
- Water, 1 cup
- Coconut milk, 1 cup
- 1 small onion, chopped
- 2 cloves garlic, minced
- 1 jalapeno pepper, seeded and diced
- Lemon juice, 2 tablespoon
- Hemp seeds, 2 tablespoon
- Extra virgin olive oil, ¼ cup
- Chopped parsley, 2 tablespoons
- Pepper and salt according to taste

Directions:

Take a bowl; combine and mix hemp seeds, lemon juice, olive oil, garlic, onion, coconut milk, water, salt, pepper, beets in it and serve with topped parsley.

Servings: 2
Preparation time: 20 min
Cooking time: 5 min

Zucchini And Cauliflower Soup

Ingredients:

- 1 young zucchini
- Cauliflower florets, 2 cups
- 1 small avocado
- Water, 1 cup
- 1 Garlic clove
- ½ small sweet onion
- Chopped cilantro, 4 tablespoons
- Cumin powder, ½ teaspoon
- 1 pinch chili flakes
- Pepper and salt to taste

Directions:

Process all the ingredients in food blender; process until creamy and serve.

Servings: 1
Preparation time: 15 min
Cooking time: 10 min

Asparagus And Mushroom Soup

Ingredients:

- 14 asparagus spears, trimmed
- 1 ripe avocado, peeled
- 1 sweet onion
- 2 clove garlic
- Water, 2 cups
- Coconut milk, ½ cup

- Olive oil, 2 tablespoons
- Chopped cilantro, 2 tablespoons
- Button mushroom, 1 cup, sliced
- Pepper and salt to taste

Directions:

1. Pulse chopped cilantro, olive oil, coconut milk, water, garlic, onion, avocado as well as asparagus in a mixer for 2 minutes or until smooth.
2. Season with salt as well as pepper and serve with chopped mushrooms onto it.

Servings: 1
Preparation time: 10 min
Cooking time: 10 min

Broccoli Soup

Ingredients:

- Broccoli florets, 2 cups
- Avocado, ½
- Celery stalk, 1
- Garlic clove, 1
- Grated ginger, ½ teaspoon
- Chopped onion, 1 tablespoon
- Water, 1 cup
- Almond milk, 1 cup
- 1 ripe tomato, peeled and diced
- Sliced almonds, 2 tablespoons
- Pepper and salt to taste

Directions:

1. Reserve almonds as well as tomato and pulse the remaining ingredients in a mixer; pulse until creamy.
2. Serve with diced tomatoes and splashed sliced almonds.

Servings: 2
Preparation time: 15 min
Cooking time: 10 min

Carrot Ginger Soup

Ingredients:

- Fresh carrot juice, 1 cup
- 2 large carrots, sliced
- Garlic clove, 1
- Garam masala, 1 teaspoon
- Grated ginger, 1 teaspoon
- Tahini paste, 1 tablespoon
- Small shallot, 1
- Water, 2 cups
- Pepper and salt to taste
- Pumpkin seed oil, 2 tablespoons

Directions:

1. Pulse carrot, garlic, carrot juice, garam masala, ginger, tahini paste, water as well as shallot together in a mixer for about 90 seconds or until creamy.
2. Season with salt as well as pepper.
3. Serve mixture with drizzled pumpkin seed oil.

Servings: 2
Preparation time: 15 min
Cooking time: 10 min

Lime Avocado Soup

Ingredients:
- Ripe avocados, peeled, 2
- Cucumber, ½
- Celery stalk, ½
- 1 handful fresh coriander
- Cumin powder, ¼ teaspoon
- Water, 1 cup
- Coconut milk, 1 ½ cups
- Coconut flesh, ¼ cup
- 2 limes, juiced
- Pepper and salt to taste
- Chopped chives, 2 tablespoons

Directions:
1. Pulse lime juice, coconut flesh, coconut milk, water, cumin powder, coriander, celery stalk, avocados as well as cucumber together in a mixer; process until creamy.
2. Season with salt as well as pepper.
3. Serve with splashed sliced chives.

Servings: 2
Preparation time: 10 min
Cooking time: 10 min

Cucumber And Cashew Soup

Ingredients:
- Cucumber, 1
- Cashew nuts, 1 cup, soaked overnight
- 4 mint leaves

- Water, 1 ½ cups
- Lemon juice, 2 tablespoons
- 1 garlic clove
- Pepper and salt to taste

Directions:
Pulse all the ingredients; process until creamy and serve.

Servings: 1
Preparation time: 5 min
Cooking time: 5 min

Cilantro And Kale Soup

Ingredients:
- 1 bunch cilantro
- 1 ripe avocado, peeled
- 1 cucumber
- 1 green onion, chopped
- 1 garlic clove, chopped
- Water, 1 ½ cups
- 4 kale leaves, shredded
- Olive oil, 2 tablespoons
- Grated ginger, 2 teaspoons
- Pepper and salt to taste

Directions:
1. Pulse garlic, cilantro, avocado, green onion, cucumber as well as water in a mixer; process until smooth.
2. Combine olive oil, ginger alongside kale in a separate shallow bowl; season with salt as well as pepper and serve onto above mixture.

Servings: 1
Preparation time: 15 min
Cooking time: 10 min

Sweet Potato Spiced Soup

Ingredients:

- 2 large sweet potatoes, peeled and cubed
- Turmeric powder, 1 teaspoon
- Cumin powder, ½ teaspoon
- 1 pinch nutmeg
- 1 pinch cinnamon powder
- Coconut cream, ½ cup
- Water, 2 cups
- Garlic powder, ¼ teaspoon
- Onion powder, ¼ teaspoon
- Hemp seeds, 4 tablespoons
- Pepper and salt to taste

Directions:

1. Pulse cinnamon, nutmeg, cumin powder, sweet potatoes, garlic, coconut cream, water as well as turmeric for 2 minutes in a mixer.
2. Season with salt as well as pepper and serve with splashed hemp seeds.

Servings: 2
Preparation time: 15 min
Cooking time: 10 min

Guacamole Soup

Ingredients:
- 3 ripe avocados
- Fresh cilantro, ½ cup
- Water, 1 cup
- Coconut milk, 1 cup
- 2 cloves garlic
- Chives, 4 tablespoons
- Pepper and salt according to taste
- 1 diced tomato

Directions:
1. Pulse water, coconut milk, cilantro, garlic, cloves, chives as well as avocados in a mixer; process well and season with pepper and salt.
2. Serve with topped tomatoes.

Servings: 2
Preparation time: 15 min
Cooking time: 10 min

Salads

Delicious Paleo Salad

Ingredients:

- One large zucchini, cubed
- 6 bacon strips
- One onion, chopped
- Mushrooms, 1 cup, sliced
- One lettuce head, leaves, torn
- Two cups arugula
- Black pepper and sea salt to the taste
- Two tablespoons maple syrup
- One teaspoon mustard
- Four tablespoons extra virgin olive oil
- Two teaspoons balsamic vinegar
- Two garlic cloves, minced

Directions:

1. Spread zucchini cubes on a lined baking sheet, sprinkle with a pinch of sea salt, pepper, drizzle balsamic vinegar and the oil, toss to coat, introduce in the oven at 400 degrees F and bake for 25 minutes.
2. Meanwhile, heat up a pan with the oil over medium heat and cook bacon strips for 7-8 minutes until crisp. Place the cooked strips on a paper towel.
3. Heat up another pan with the oil over medium heat and fry onions for 1-2 minutes.
4. Add mushrooms, salt and pepper and cook until brown.
5. In a salad bowl, mix lettuce leaves, arugula, roasted zucchini, mushroom mixture and bacon strips.

6. In a small bowl, mix maple syrup with balsamic vinegar, mustard, garlic and olive oil and whisk very well.
7. Pour this over salad, toss to coat and serve.

Servings: 2
Preparation time: 15 min
Cooking time: 35 min

Advanced Avocado Tuna Salad

Ingredients:
- 1 avocado
- Salt and pepper to taste
- Cooked tuna, 5 ounces
- Chopped tomatoes, 1 cup
- Chopped onion, 1 tablespoon
- 1 Lemon, juiced

Directions:
1. Scoop avocado's flesh into a bowl; mash together with tomatoes, lemon juice alongside onion.
2. Stir in tuna, salt as well as pepper; stuff the mixture into avocados and serve.

Servings: 1
Preparation time: 25 min
Cooking time: 15 min

Chicken Eastern Surprise

Ingredients

For Salad:

- Grilled chicken, 2 cups, chopped
- 6 baby bok choy, grilled and chopped
- 2 green onions, chopped
- Cilantro, ¼ cup , chopped
- Sesame seeds, 1 tablespoon
- Pepper and salt to taste

For Dressing:

- Fresh lime juice, 2 tablespoons
- Sesame oil, 1 tablespoon
- Coconut cream, 2 tablespoons
- Fresh ginger, 1 teaspoon

Directions:

1. Mix together sesame seeds, cilantro, onions, pepper, salt, chicken as well as bok choy in a bowl.
2. Pulse dressing ingredients in a mixer; blend until creamy and toss with salad.
3. Refrigerate for an hour and serve with topped sesame seeds.

Servings: 2
Preparation time: 30 min
Cooking time: 1 h 10 min

Creamy Carrot Salad

Ingredients:
- Carrot, 1 pound, shredded
- Crushed pineapples, 20 ounces, drained
- Chicken breast, boiled and shredded
- Flaked coconut, ¾ cup
- Coconut milk, 8 ounces

Directions:
1. Combine all ingredients in a bowl and toss to mix.
2. Refrigerate and serve.

Servings: 4
Preparation time: 35 min
Cooking time: 15 min

Asian Aspiration Salad

Ingredients:
- 1 red bell pepper, sliced
- 1 cucumber, cut into half and sliced
- 1 large carrot, cut into matchsticks
- 2 boiled eggs
- Fresh ginger juice and vinegar

Directions:
Take a bowl, add all ingredients together, mix and serve.

Servings: 1
Preparation time: 20 min
Cooking time: 5 min

Paleo Shrimp Salad

Ingredients:

- 5 cups mixed greens
- ½ cup cherry tomatoes, cut into halves
- 1 pound shrimp, peeled and deveined
- 1 small red onion, thinly sliced
- 1 avocado, pitted, peeled and chopped
- Black pepper to the taste
- ½ tablespoon sweet paprika
- ½ teaspoon cumin
- 1 tablespoon chili powder
- 1/3 cup cilantro, finely chopped
- ½ cup lime juice
- ¼ cup extra virgin olive oil

Directions:

1. In a bowl, mix chili powder with cumin, paprika, ¼ cup lime juice and shrimp, toss to coat and leave aside for 20 minutes.
2. Place shrimps on preheated grill over medium-high heat, cook for 4 minutes on each side and transfer to a bowl.
3. In a small bowl, mix cilantro with oil, the rest of the lime juice and pepper to the taste and whisk very well.
4. In a large salad bowl, mix greens with tomatoes, onion, avocado, and shrimp.
5. Add salad dressing, toss to coat and serve right away.

Servings: 2
Preparation time: 20 min
Cooking time: 15 min

Macadamia Chicken Salad

Ingredients:

- Olive oil, 1 tablespoon
- Vinegar, 2 teaspoons
- Julienned basil, 2 tablespoons
- Diced celery, ½ cup
- Macadamia nuts, ½ cup, chopped
- Few pinches of pepper and low sodium salt
- Macadamia nut oil, 1 teaspoon
- Organic chicken breast, 1 lb
- Lemon juice, 1 tablespoon

Directions:

1. Prepare oven at 350 F.
2. Bake chicken (seasoned with pepper and salt) in oven for 30 minutes or until golden.
3. Chill for a while and shred chicken in a bowl; add pepper, salt, nuts, celery, dressing as well as basil and stir before serving.

Servings: 2
Preparation time: 40 min
Cooking time: 10 min

Spicy Tuna Salad

Ingredients:

- Tuna, 2 cans, water packed, drained
- Black olives, 1 cup, chopped
- Green olives, 1 cup, chopped
- 2 green onions, chopped

- 1 jalapeno pepper, finely chopped
- Capers, 3 tablespoons, rinsed
- Red chili flakes, ½ teaspoon
- 2 lemon, juiced
- Splash of olive oil
- 1 head butter lettuce, kale or mixed greens
- 1 avocado, sliced

Directions:
Combine lemon juice, chili flakes, caper, jalapeno pepper, onions, tuna, green olives as well as black olives; add chopped avocado as well as greens topping to it and serve.

Servings: 2
Preparation time: 15 min
Cooking time: 10 min

Paleo Eggplant and Tomato Salad
Ingredients
For Salad:
- ½ cup sun-dried tomatoes, sliced
- One eggplant, sliced
- One green onion, sliced
- Black pepper to the taste
- 4 cups mixed salad greens
- One tablespoon mint leaves, finely chopped
- One tablespoon oregano, finely chopped
- One tablespoon parsley leaves, finely chopped
- Four tablespoons extra virgin olive oil

For Dressing:

- Two garlic cloves, minced
- ¼ cup extra virgin olive oil
- ½ tablespoon mustard
- One tablespoon lemon juice
- ½ teaspoon smoked paprika
- A pinch of sea salt
- Black pepper to the taste

Directions:

1. Brush eggplant cuts with olive oil, season with dark pepper, put them on preheated barbecue over medium-high warmth, cook for 3 minutes on each side and exchange them for a serving of mixed greens bowl.
2. Add sun-dried tomatoes, onion, greens, mint, parsley, oregano, and pepper to the taste and four tablespoons olive oil and toss to coat.
3. In a small bowl, mix ¼ cup olive oil with garlic, mustard, paprika, lemon juice, salt, and pepper to the taste and whisk very well.
4. Pour this over salad, toss to coat gently and serve.

Servings: 4
Preparation time: 10 min
Cooking time: 8 min
Nutritional value: calories 130, fat 27, carbs 14, fiber 2, protein 4

Chicken Salad

Ingredients

For Salad:
- Organic chicken, 2 cups, cooked
- Fresh mint, ¼ cup , chopped
- Fresh cilantro, ¼ cup, chopped
- Radishes, ¼ cup, julienned
- Scallions, ¼ cup, trimmed and julienned
- Carrot, 1 cup, julienned
- 1 small head of cabbage, shredded

For Vinaigrette:
- Fresh ginger, 1 teaspoon
- 1 clove garlic, crushed
- 1 chipotle pepper
- Sesame oil, 2 tablespoons
- ½ lime, juiced
- Vinegar, 2 tablespoons

Directions:
1. Combine cabbage, carrot, scallions as well as radishes together.
2. Add splashed chicken, mint as well as cilantro and keep it aside.
3. Prepare vinaigrette by mixing all ingredients and moisten salad with vinaigrette before serving.

Servings: 2
Preparation time: 30 min
Cooking time: 10 min

Artichoke Tuna Delight

Ingredients:

- Diced grilled tuna, 1 ½ cups
- 1 small carrot julienned and cut into small pieces
- Finely diced red onion, ¼ cup
- 5 artichoke hearts, diced
- Capers, 2 tablespoons
- 6 radicchio leaves
- Pepper and salt to taste

Directions:

1. Reserve radicchio leaves and combine the rest of ingredients in a shallow bowl.
2. Toss to mix and scatter on radicchio leaves; refrigerate for a while and serve.

Servings: 1
Preparation time: 25 min
Cooking time: 20 min

Avocado Chicken Salad

Ingredients:

- Chicken breast, cooked and chopped
- Lettuce leaves of your choice
- Pepper and salt according to taste
- Mashed avocado
- Chopped almonds

Directions:

1. Reserve lettuce; combine rest of the ingredients and season with salt as well as pepper.
2. Scatter mixture onto lettuce leaves and roll it up before serving.

Servings: 1
Preparation time: 30 min
Cooking time: 10 min

Paleo Pork Salad

Ingredients:

- 2 lettuce heads, torn
- 2 cups pork, already cooked and shredded
- 1 avocado, pitted, peeled and chopped
- 1 cup cherry tomatoes, cut into halves
- 1 green bell pepper, sliced
- 2 green onions, thinly sliced
- A pinch of sea salt
- Black pepper to the taste
- Juice of 1 medium lime
- 1 tablespoon apple cider vinegar
- 3 tablespoons extra virgin olive oil

Directions:

1. In a small bowl, mix oil with lime juice, vinegar and black pepper and whisk well.
2. Heat up a pan over medium heat, add pork meat and heat it up.
3. Meanwhile, in a salad bowl, mix lettuce leaves with tomatoes, bell pepper, avocado and green onions.

4. Add pork, drizzle the dressing, toss to coat and serve.

Servings: 4
Preparation time: 10 min
Cooking time: 5 min
Nutritional value: calories 322, fat 45, carbs 23, fiber 4, protein 36

Chicken Basil Avocado Salad

Ingredients:
- Basil leaves, ½ cup, stem removed
- 1 cooked boneless and skinless chicken breast, shredded
- Cherry tomatoes, 1 cup, sliced
- Extra virgin olive oil, 2 tablespoons
- 2 small avocados, skin removed
- Low sodium salt, ½ teaspoon
- Ground black pepper, 1/8 teaspoon

Directions:
1. Arrange shredded chicken and tomatoes in a bowl.
2. Pulse olive oil, salt, black pepper, basil as well as avocados in a mixer; process until creamy and decant onto tomatoes and chicken.
3. Toss, refrigerate and serve.

Servings: 2
Preparation time: 25 min
Cooking time: 15 min

Kale and Avocado Salad

Ingredients:

- 2 tablespoons olive oil
- 1 teaspoon maple syrup
- 3 tablespoons lemon juice
- 2 basil leaves, chopped
- 1 garlic clove, minced
- 1 avocado, pitted, peeled and cut
- 1 bunch kale, chopped
- 1 cup grapes, seedless and halved
- ¼ cup pumpkin seeds
- 1/3 cup red onion, chopped

Directions:

1. In a salad bowl, mix kale with avocado, grapes, pumpkin seeds and onion and stir.
2. In another bowl, combine oil with maple syrup, lemon juice, basil and garlic and whisk well.
3. Add this to salad, toss to coat and serve.

Servings: 2
Preparation time: 10 min
Cooking time: 10 min
Nutritional value: calories 120, fat 1, fiber 1, carbs 2, protein 11

Mediterranean Chicken Delish Salad

Ingredients:

- 1 lemon, juiced
- 1 red onion, diced
- 1 head of romaine or butter lettuce
- Salt and pepper according to taste
- Fresh cilantro, ¼ cup , chopped
- Olive oil, ½ cup
- 1 roasted chicken, shredded

Directions:

Add salt, pepper, lemon, red onion, cilantro as well as oil to shredded chicken in a bowl; mix and enjoy over lettuce boat.

Servings: 2
Preparation time: 25 min
Cooking time: 10 min

Main Dishes

Special Paleo Pork Chops

Ingredients:

- Eight sage springs
- Four pork chops, bone-in
- Four tablespoons ghee
- Four garlic cloves, crushed
- One tablespoon coconut oil
- A pinch of sea salt
- Black pepper to the taste

Directions:

1. Season pork chops with a pinch of sea salt and pepper to the taste.
2. Heat up a pan with the oil over medium-high heat, add pork chops and cook for 10 minutes turning them often.
3. Take pork chops off heat, add ghee, sage, and garlic and toss to coat.
4. Return to heat, cook for 4 minutes often stirring, divide between plates and serve.

Servings: 4
Preparation time: 10 min
Cooking time: 30 min
Nutritional value: calories 250, fat 41, carbs 1, fiber 1, sugar 0.1, protein 18.3

Great Beef Teriyaki

Ingredients:

- Two green onions, chopped
- 1 and ½ pounds steaks, sliced
- ¼ cup honey
- ½ cup coconut aminos
- One tablespoon ginger, minced
- One tablespoon coconut flour
- One tablespoon water
- Two garlic cloves, minced
- ¼ cup pear juice
- Some bacon fat
- Four tablespoons white wine

Directions:

1. Heat up a pan with the bacon fat over medium heat, add ginger and garlic, stir and cook for 2 minutes. Add wine, stir and cook until it evaporates.
2. Add honey, aminos, pear juice, stir, bring to a simmer and cook for 12 minutes.
3. Add coconut flour mixed with the water, stir and cook until it thickens.
4. Heat up another pan with some bacon fat over medium-high heat, add steak slices and brown them for 2 minutes on each side.
5. Add green onions and half of the sauce you've just made, stir gently and cook for 3 minutes more.
6. Divide steaks between plates and serve with the rest of the sauce on top.

Servings: 4

Preparation time: 10 min

Cooking time: 20 min

Nutritional value: calories 170, fat 3, fiber 2, carbs 2, protein 8

Italian Pulled Pork Ragu

Ingredients:

- 18 ounces pork tenderloin
- One teaspoon sea salt
- Black pepper to taste
- One teaspoon olive oil
- Five cloves garlic, smashed with the side of a knife
- 4 cups of finely chopped tomatoes
- Roasted red bell peppers, 7 ounces
- 2 sprigs fresh thyme
- Two bay leaves
- One tablespoon chopped fresh parsley, divided

Directions:

1. Sprinkle the pork tenderloin with salt and pepper.
2. Smash garlic cloves with the side of a knife.
3. Add oil to a preheated large pot or Dutch oven.
4. Add garlic and sauté over medium-high heat for about 1 to 1 ½ minutes, until golden. Remove the garlic with a slotted spoon and set aside.
5. Add pork and brown it on each side for about 2 minutes.
6. Add tomatoes, red bell peppers, fresh thyme, bay leaves and half of the chopped parsley. Bring to a boil, cover, and

cook on low for about 2 hours, until the pork is fork tender.

7. Remove bay leaves and shred the pork with two forks.
8. Serve.

Servings: 4
Preparation time: 15 min
Cooking time: 2 h 15 min

Spicy Slow-Cooked Chicken Wings

Ingredients:
- Chicken wings, 2 pounds
- Red chili flakes, 1 teaspoon
- Tomato paste, ½ can
- Water, ½ cup
- Maple syrup, ½ cup
- Garlic powder, 1 tablespoon
- Cayenne, 1 teaspoon
- Oregano, 1 teaspoon

Directions:
1. Combine and mix chili flakes, tomato paste, water, maple syrup, garlic powder, cayenne, oregano in a shallow bowl.
2. Add chicken to it; transfer it to slow cooker and cook for 4 hours before serving.

Servings: 2
Preparation time: 10 min
Cooking time: 4 h

Apricot Walnut Chicken

Ingredients:

- Extra virgin olive oil, 1 teaspoon
- Rosemary, 1 teaspoon
- Sea salt, 1 teaspoon
- Walnuts, ½ cups , chopped
- 6 apricots
- Chicken broth, 2 cups
- Chicken breast, 1 pound , skinless, boneless and cubed

Directions:

1. Boil apricots and peel.
2. Add chicken breast, chicken broth, apricots, walnuts, sea salt, rosemary to slow cooker coated with olive oil, cook for 4 hours on medium-high heat and serve.

Servings: 2
Preparation time: 20 min
Cooking time: 4 h

Kale Orange Chicken

Ingredients:

- Chicken breast, 1 pound, skinless, boneless and cubed
- Fresh orange juice, ½ cup
- Water, ½ cup
- Coconut aminos, ¼ cup
- Flax seeds, 3 tablespoons
- Kale, 3 cups, chopped
- Sea salt, 1 teaspoon
- Cracked black pepper, 1 teaspoon

Directions:
Put all ingredients to a slow cooker; set medium-high heat and cook for about 4 hours before serving.

Servings: 2
Preparation time: 25 min
Cooking time: 4 h

Spinach Beef Pie

Ingredients

For Crust:
- Raw almonds, 1 cup
- Coconut oil, 2 tablespoons
- 2 kale leaves
- Nutritional yeast, 1 tablespoon (optional)
- Dried basil, 1 teaspoon
- 1 pinch low sodium salt

For Filling:
- Cashews, 1 ½ cups, soaked overnight
- 2 garlic cloves
- Lemon juice, 2 tablespoons
- Spinach leaves, 3 cups
- Coconut oil, 4 tablespoons
- 4 beef slices, grilled
- Pepper and salt to taste
- Sun dried tomatoes, 1 cup

Directions:

1. Pulse all crust ingredients in a mixer and press in a pie. Add beef slices onto it.
2. Now pulse cashew nuts, garlic, lemon juice, spinach as well as coconut oil to prepare filling. Season with pepper as well as salt; decant onto crust alongside tomatoes.
3. Refrigerate for 60 minutes before serving.

Servings: 4
Preparation time: 35 min
Cooking time: 1 h

Chicken Spicy "Rice"

Ingredients:

- 4 cooked chicken fillets, cubed
- 1 head cauliflower, cut into florets
- Nutritional yeast, 4 tablespoons (optional)
- Vinegar, 1 teaspoon
- Chopped dill, 2 tablespoons
- Olive oil, 4 tablespoons
- Pepper and salt to taste

Directions:

1. Process cauliflower in a mixer to the size of rice.
2. Spoon in dill, olive oil, pepper, salt, yeast, chicken as well as vinegar and serve.

Servings: 4
Preparation time: 35 min
Cooking time: 10 min

Beef Stew

Ingredients:

- One red onion, chopped
- One tablespoon balsamic vinegar
- Two tablespoons coconut oil
- A pinch of sea salt
- 1 pound beef, ground
- ¼ cup pine nuts
- Three garlic cloves, minced
- 2/3 teaspoon ginger, grated
- One teaspoon coriander seeds
- One teaspoon cumin, ground
- One teaspoon paprika
- 1 and ½ cups veggie stock
- One carrot, chopped
- 2/3 cup canned tomatoes, chopped
- ¼ cup parsley, chopped
- Zest of 1 lemon, grated

Directions:

1. Heat up a pot with the oil over medium heat, add onion and a pinch of salt, stir and cook for 10 minutes.
2. Add vinegar, stir and cook for 1 minute more.
3. Heat up another pan over medium heat, add pine nuts, stir, toast for 2 minutes and transfer to a bowl.
4. Add ginger and meat to onions, stir and cook for 2 minutes.
5. Add garlic, coriander, cumin, and paprika, stir and cook for 2 minutes.

6. Add pine nuts, stock, carrot, tomatoes and lemon zest, stir, cover and cook for 20 minutes.
7. Add parsley, stir, cook for 2 minutes more, divide into bowls and serve.

Servings: 4
Preparation time: 10 min
Cooking time: 35 min
Nutritional value: calories 200, fat 5, fiber 3, carbs 6, protein 10

Paleo Beef Stir Fry

Ingredients:
- 10 ounces mushrooms, sliced
- 10 ounces asparagus, sliced
- 1 and ½ pounds beef steak, thinly sliced
- Two tablespoons honey
- 1/3 cup coconut amino
- Two teaspoons apple cider vinegar
- ½ teaspoon ginger, minced
- Six garlic cloves, minced
- One chili, sliced
- One tablespoon coconut oil
- Black pepper to the taste

Directions:
1. In a bowl, mix garlic with coconut amino, honey, ginger, and vinegar and whisk well.
2. Put some water in a pan, heat up over medium-high heat, add asparagus and black pepper, cook for 3 minutes,

transfer to a bowl filled with ice water, drain and leave aside.

3. Heat up a pan with the oil over medium-high heat, add mushrooms, cook for 2 minutes on each side, transfer to a bowl and also leave aside.

4. Heat up the same pan over high heat, add meat, brown for a few minutes and mix with chili pepper.

5. Cook for two more minutes and mix with asparagus, mushrooms and vinegar sauce you've made at the beginning.

6. Stir well, cook for 3 minutes, take off heat, divide between plates and serve.

Servings: 4
Preparation time: 10 min
Cooking time: 20 min
Nutritional value: calories 165, fat 7.2, carbs 6.33, fiber 1.3, sugar 3, protein 18.4

Amazing Beef Lasagna

Ingredients:
- One red bell pepper, chopped
- One eggplant, sliced lengthwise
- Two zucchinis, sliced lengthwise
- 1 pound beef, ground
- 2 cups tomatoes, chopped
- Two teaspoons oregano, dried
- ¼ cup basil, chopped
- Two garlic cloves, minced
- One yellow onion, chopped

- One tablespoon parsley, chopped
- Two tablespoons olive oil
- A pinch of sea salt
- Black pepper to the taste

Directions:
1. Heat up a pan with the oil over medium-high heat, add onion and garlic, stir and cook for 2 minutes.
2. Add beef, stir and brown for 5 minutes more.
3. Add bell pepper, tomatoes, oregano, basil, and parsley, stir and cook for 4 minutes more.
4. Add black pepper to the taste and a pinch of salt and stir well again.
5. Arrange layers of eggplant and zucchini slices with the sauce you've made in your slow cooker.
6. Cover and cook on Low for 4 hours and 45 minutes.
7. Divide your lasagna between plates and serve.

Servings: 6
Preparation time: 10 min
Cooking time: 5 h 15 min
Nutritional value: calories 240, fat 10, fiber 5, carbs 7, protein 12

Hawaiian Pineapple Chicken

Ingredients:
- Chicken breast, 1 pound, boneless, skinless and cubed
- Ginger, 1 tablespoon
- 1 red onion, diced
- 1 jalapeno, diced
- Lime juice, 1 tablespoon

- Coriander leaves, ½ cup
- Pineapple, ¾ cup
- Extra virgin olive oil, 1 teaspoon

Directions:
1. Add chicken cubes to slow cooker coated with olive oil.
2. Cook for 4 hours on high-heat with topped remaining ingredients and serve.

Servings: 2
Preparation time: 20 min
Cooking time: 4 h

Pesto Chicken

Ingredients:
- Chicken breast, 1 pound, boneless and skinless
- 1 onion, peeled and sliced
- 4 cloves garlic, chopped
- 1 red bell pepper, sliced
- Basil, 2 cups
- Cashews, 1/3 cup
- Pine nuts, ¼ cup
- Low sodium salt, ½ teaspoon
- Pepper, ½ teaspoon
- Extra virgin olive oil, 1 tablespoon

Directions:

1. To prepare sauce: pulse oil, salt, pine nuts, cashews, basil, pepper, garlic as well as onion together in a mixer.
2. Add chicken and red bell pepper to slow cooker coated with half the sauce and decant remaining sauce onto chicken.
3. Serve after cooking for 4 hours on high-heat.

Servings: 2
Preparation time: 15 min
Cooking time: 4 h

Eggie Vegetable Stir-Fry

Ingredients:

- Butternut squash, 1 pound, peeled and cut into 1 inch cube
- 3 eggs, beaten
- Coconut oil, 1 tablespoon
- Black pepper, ½ teaspoon
- Low sodium salt, ½ teaspoon
- 1 small yellow onion, sliced
- 3 garlic cloves, minced
- Eggplants, 1 ½ pounds, slice into 1 inch thick pieces
- 3 baby bok choy stems, cut into 1 inch pieces
- 3 baby bok choy leaves, sliced thinly

Directions:

1. Add onions to a pan coated with oil; fry onions for 2 minutes or until light brown.
2. Add garlic and cook for one more minute.
3. Now add salt, pepper, bok choy stems, butternut squash and eggplant; cook un-wrapped for additional 12 minutes.

72

4. After adding bok choy leaves cook for last 4 minutes; include beaten eggs while cooking and serve.

Servings: 4
Preparation time: 25 min
Cooking time: 20 min

Tasty Paleo Pulled Pork

Ingredients:
- ½ cup beef stock
- 2 cups chopped tomatoes
- 2 pounds organic pork shoulder
- Two green chili peppers, chopped
- One tablespoon garlic powder
- One tablespoon chili powder
- One teaspoon onion powder
- One teaspoon cumin
- One teaspoon paprika
- Black pepper and salt to the taste

Directions:
1. In a bowl, mix chili powder with onion and garlic one.
2. Add cumin, paprika, salt and pepper to the taste and stir everything.
3. Add pork, rub well and keep in the fridge for 12 hours.
4. Transfer pork to your slow cooker, add stock, tomatoes and green chili peppers, stir, cover and cook on Low for 8 hours.
5. Transfer pork to a plate, leave aside to cool down and shred.

6. Strain sauce from slow cooker into a pan, bring to a boil over medium heat and simmer for 8 minutes stirring all the time.
7. Add shredded pork to the sauce, stir, reduce heat to medium and cook for 20 more minutes.
8. Divide between plates and serve hot.

Servings: 4
Preparation time: 12 h 10 min
Cooking time: 8 h 30 min
Nutritional value: calories 250, fat 35, carbs 5, fiber 2, protein 50

Italian Chicken On Cauliflower

Ingredients:
- Chicken breast, 1 pound, boneless and skinless
- Frozen cauliflower florets, 5 cups
- 2 onions, peeled and sliced
- 2 green bell peppers, seeded and sliced
- Tomatoes, 1 cup, chopped
- Sea salt, 1 teaspoon
- Oregano, 1 tablespoon
- Garlic powder, 1 tablespoon

Directions:
1. Add chicken breast with topped cauliflower, salt as well as spices to slow cooker.
2. Add other ingredients as well and cook for 240 minutes on high-heat before you serve.

Servings: 2
Preparation time: 20 min
Cooking time: 4 h

Pomegranate Ginger Chicken

Ingredients:

- Chicken breast, 1 pound, boneless, skinless
- 2 red bell peppers, seeded and diced
- Pomegranate juice, ½ cup
- Low sodium chicken stock, 1 cup
- Grated ginger, 2 tablespoons
- Onion powder, 1 tablespoon
- Thyme, ½ teaspoon
- Low sodium salt, 1 teaspoon
- Pepper, 1 teaspoon
- Extra virgin olive oil, 1 teaspoon

Directions:

Add all the ingredients to slow cooker coated with olive oil; cook for 240 minutes on high-heat and serve.

Servings: 2
Preparation time: 10 min
Cooking time: 4 h

Paleo Salmon Pie

Ingredients:

- Eight sweet potatoes, thinly sliced
- 4 cups salmon, already cooked and shredded
- One red onion, chopped

- Two carrots, cut
- One celery stalk, cut
- A pinch of sea salt
- Black pepper to the taste
- Two tablespoons chives, chopped
- 2 cups coconut milk
- One tablespoon tapioca starch
- Two garlic cloves, minced
- Three tablespoons ghee

Directions:
1. Heat up a pan with the ghee over medium heat, add garlic and tapioca, stir and cook for 1 minute.
2. Add coconut milk, stir and cook for 3 minutes.
3. Add a pinch of sea salt and pepper and stir again.
4. In a bowl, mix carrots with salmon, celery, chives, onion, and pepper to the taste and stir well.
5. Arrange a layer of potatoes in a baking dish, add some of the coconut sauce, add half of the salmon mix, the rest of the vegetables and top with the remaining sauce.
6. Introduce in the oven at 375 degrees F and bake for 1 hour.
7. Divide between plates and serve hot.

Servings: 4
Preparation time: 15 min
Cooking time: 1 h
Nutritional value: calories 260, fat 11, carbs 20, fiber 12, protein 14

Veggies and Side Dishes
Cauliflower With Curry Sauce

Ingredients:

- Cauliflower, cut into florets, 1 head
- Zucchini, 1
- Curry powder, 1 teaspoon
- Cashews, soaked overnight, ¼ cup
- Lemon juice, 2 tablespoons
- Turmeric, ½ teaspoon
- Garlic powder, 1 teaspoon
- Onion powder, 1 teaspoon
- Smoked paprika, ½ teaspoon
- Coconut milk, ¼ cup
- Olive oil, 2 tablespoons
- Pepper and salt to taste

Directions:

1. Pulse pepper, salt, olive oil, paprika, coconut milk, garlic powder, onion powder, turmeric, cashews, lemon juice, zucchini as well as curry powder in food processor; process until creamy.
2. Spread the mixture gently onto cauliflower florets and serve.

Servings: 4
Preparation time: 5 min
Cooking time: 15 min

Mint Zucchini Pasta With Pistachio Crumble

Ingredients:
- Lemon zest, 1 teaspoon
- Pistachio, ½ cup
- Almonds, ½ cup
- 1 pinch chili flakes
- Pepper and salt accordingly
- 4 zucchinis, sliced finely
- 4 mint leaves
- Olive oil, 2 tablespoons
- Lemon juice, 2 tablespoons
- 2 garlic cloves
- ½ shallot

Directions:
1. Pulse salt, pepper, lemon juice, lemon zest, mint, olive oil, garlic as well as shallots in a mixer; arrange mixture on platters alongside zucchinis.
2. Now pulse pistachio as well as almonds in food blender; season with chili flakes, salt, pepper and serve with splashed pasta.

Servings: 4
Preparation time: 10 min
Cooking time: 10 min

Guacamole Stuffed Peppers

Ingredients:

- 2 large bell peppers, halved and then cored
- 1 ripe avocado
- 2 garlic cloves
- 1 green onion
- Chopped cilantro, 4 tablespoons
- 6 cherry tomatoes, diced
- Pepper and salt to taste
- 1 pinch chili flakes
- Lime juice, 2 tablespoons

Directions:

1. Pulse avocado, garlic, onion, lemon juice, chili flakes, pepper, salt as well as cilantro in a mixer; process until creamy.
2. Fill in tomatoes and stir in halved bell peppers before serving.

Servings: 2
Preparation time: 10 min
Cooking time: 15 min

Sweet Apple Coleslaw

Ingredients:

- Finely sliced white cabbage, 2 cups
- 2 medium sized carrots, shredded
- 1 apple, chopped
- 1 stalk celery, chopped

- 1 green onion, sliced thinly
- Handful of toasted sunflower seeds
- Extra virgin olive oil, ¼ cup
- Organic honey, 2 tablespoons
- Freshly squeezed lemon juice, 1 tablespoon
- Ground black pepper and sea salt to taste

Directions:
1. Shake salt, pepper, olive oil, lemon juice as well as honey together in jar to make coleslaw.
2. Combine and mix veggies; toss with dressing onto it alongside splashed sunflower seeds.
3. Set aside for 15 minute before serving.

Servings: 2
Preparation time: 20 min
Cooking time: 20 min

Vegetable Raw Pie

Ingredients
For Crust:
- Almonds, 2 cups
- Cashews, ½ cup , soaked overnight
- Coconut oil, 2 tablespoons
- 1 pinch low sodium salt
- Cumin powder, ¼ teaspoon

For Filling:
- Arugula leaves, 2 cups
- Shredded lettuce, 2 cups
- 1 avocado, peeled and sliced
- 1 garlic clove
- 1 green onion
- Chopped parsley, 2 tablespoons
- 1 lime, juiced
- Cherry tomatoes, 1 cup, halved
- Pepper and salt to taste

Directions:
1. Pulse almonds, cashews, coconut oil, salt, cumin powder in a mixer; place it in pie tin and reserve.
2. Prepare filling by combining avocado, garlic, green onion, parsley as well as lime juice; season with pepper as well as salt.
3. Mix lettuce, arugula as well as avocado sauce and decant onto crust.
4. Serve with splashed cherry tomatoes.

Servings: 2
Preparation time: 10 min
Cooking time: 20 min

Parsnip "Rice" With Hemp Seed And Basil

Ingredients:
- Parsnip, 1 pound, peeled and sliced
- Hemp seeds, 2 tablespoons
- 1 pinch low sodium salt

- Chopped basil, 4 tablespoons
- 2 ripe tomatoes, cubed
- Pepper according to taste
- Olive oil, 2 tablespoons

Directions:
1. Pulse parsnip, salt as well as hemp seeds in a mixer; blend to the shape of rice.
2. Combine with salt, pepper, basil, tomatoes as well as olive oil in a bowl and serve.

Servings: 2
Preparation time: 10 min
Cooking time: 10 min

Avocado And Tomato Stacks

Ingredients:
- 2 ripe tomatoes, sliced
- 1 ripe avocado, peeled and sliced
- 2 garlic cloves
- Cilantro leaves, 1 cup
- Extra virgin olive oil, ¼ cup
- 1 pinch chili flakes
- Pepper and salt according to taste
- Lime juice, 2 tablespoons

Directions:

1. Pulse cilantro, garlic, olive oil as well as chili flakes in a mixer; flavor with pepper as well as salt.
2. Prepare avocado with splashed lime juice, cilantro sauce as well as tomato slices and serve.

Servings: 1
Preparation time: 15 min
Cooking time: 10 min

Mushroom Sauté

Ingredients:

- 1 onion, chopped
- Shiitake mushroom, 1 pound, chopped
- Coconut oil, 2 teaspoons
- Sea salt to taste
- Handful of coriander leave

Directions:

1. Sauté onion in a pan coated with coconut oil.
2. Cook mushroom in it for 12 minutes. Wrap the pan and cook mushrooms for 10 more minutes on low heat.
3. Serve with garnished coriander leaves.

Servings: 1
Preparation time: 10 min
Cooking time: 25 min

Egg Bok Choy And Basil Stir Fry

Ingredients:

- 1 lime, juiced
- Handful of fresh basil leaves, chopped
- Bok Choy greens, 1 cup, sliced thinly
- Bok Choy stems, 1 cup, sliced thinly
- 2 red chili peppers, sliced crosswise
- 1 small onion, finely chopped
- Olive oil, 2 tablespoons
- 3 eggs
- Salt according to taste

Directions:

1. Fry onions in a pan coated with olive oil.
2. Add bok choy stems and cook for 1 more minute.
3. After adding beaten eggs prepare for 2 minutes and spoon frequently.
4. Add bok choy greens, lime juice, chili peppers, salt as well as basil and cook until wilted before serving.

Servings: 2
Preparation time: 15 min
Cooking time: 10 min

Vegetarian Curry With Squash

Ingredients:

- 1 onion, chopped
- Coconut oil, 1 tablespoon
- 1 green bell pepper, sliced thinly

84

- A piece of fresh ginger, peeled and minced
- Coconut milk, 14 ounce
- 1 large acorn squash, seeded, peeled and cut into cubes
- Mixed raw nuts, 2 cups
- 1 medium yellow onion, diced
- Salt, 1 teaspoon
- 4 cloves garlic, minced
- Lime juice, 2 teaspoons
- Curry powder, 1 teaspoon
- Cilantro, ¼ cup, chopped

Directions:

1. Fry onions in a skillet coated with oil until brown.
2. Add bell pepper, ginger, garlic as well as salt and prepare for 60 more seconds.
3. Add curry powder, spoon and cook for 60 additional seconds.
4. Simmer after adding coconut milk.
5. Add squash; spoon in intervals and simmer for 18 minutes.
6. Splash roasted and crisped nuts onto curry.
7. Add lime juice after separating pan from the heat and serve with splashed cilantro.

Servings: 4
Preparation time: 20 min
Cooking time: 25 min

Tasty Carrot Salad

Ingredients:
- Olive oil, 2 tablespoons
- Lemon juice, 2 teaspoons
- Low sodium salt, ¼ teaspoon
- Mustard seeds, 1 tablespoon
- 5 carrots, medium
- 1 grated egg

Directions:
1. Toss grated carrots with salt in a bowl and keep it aside.
2. Add mustard seeds to skillet coated with olive oil and pour onto carrot when pops up. Toss and mix well with lemon juice.
3. Serve with grated eggs.

Servings: 1
Preparation time: 15 min
Cooking time: 10 min

Delicious Slaw

Ingredients:
- ½ head of cabbage, chopped
- 4 carrots, grated
- 1 onion, chopped
- Walnut oil, 3 tablespoons
- 1 egg
- Fresh lemon juice, 1 tablespoon
- Pepper and salt according to taste

Directions:

1. Combine cabbage, onion as well as grated carrot together and toss to mix.
2. To prepare dressing beat egg with walnut oil, lemon juice, salt and pepper.
3. Scatter the dressing onto salad before serving.

Servings: 4
Preparation time: 20 min
Cooking time: 10 min

Arugula Avocado And Raisins Salad

Ingredients:

- 2 handfuls of arugula leaves, washed and dried well
- 1 avocado, cut into half, seeded and sliced thinly
- Organic raisins, ½ cup
- ½ thinly sliced Spanish onion
- 6 cherry tomatoes, cut lengthwise
- Extra virgin olive oil, 6 tablespoons
- Freshly squeezed lemon juice, 2 tablespoons
- Salt and pepper to taste

Directions:

1. Prepare dressing by mixing olive oil, salt, pepper and lemon juice.
2. Combine arugula leaves, avocado, raisins, onion as well as tomatoes and serve with topped dressing.

Servings: 1
Preparation time: 15 min
Cooking time: 10 min

Pomegranate Salad

Ingredients:

- 1 arugula lettuce, washed, dried and torn into small pieces
- 1 pomegranate, seeds removed
- Extra virgin olive oil, 5 tablespoons
- 2 garlic cloves, minced
- Freshly squeezed lemon juice, 2 tablespoons
- Sea salt and pepper to taste

Directions:

1. Add oil, salt, pepper, garlic as well as lemon juice to a jar and shake to mix.
2. Mix lettuce with pomegranate seeds; decant dressing onto salad and serve.

Servings: 1
Preparation time: 10 min
Cooking time: 10 min

Black Olive Tapenade In Zucchini Boats

Ingredients:

- 3 young zucchinis
- 2 Sun-dried tomatoes
- Olive oil, 2 tablespoons
- Pitted black olives, 1 cup
- Almonds, ½ cup
- 2 basil leaves
- Pepper and salt accordingly

Directions:
1. Halve zucchinis; take the flesh out and slice. Transfer it to a bowl and keep it aside.
2. Pulse olive oil, sun-dried tomatoes, black olives, almond alongside basil leaves in a food processor and blend well. Add zucchini flesh to it; fill the mixture inside zucchini and serve.

Servings: 3
Preparation time: 10 min
Cooking time: 15 min

Paleo Desserts

Coconut Goji Berry Truffles

Ingredients:

- Coconut butter, melted, ½ cup
- Coconut, shredded, 1 cup
- Goji berries, chopped, ¼ cup
- Raw honey, 2 tablespoons
- 1 pinch salt

Directions:

1. Pulse butter, coconut, berries, salt as well as honey in the mixer.
2. Make balls of the mixture when it's firm.
3. Use candy peppers, chill and serve.

Servings: 2
Preparation time: 5 min
Cooking time: 15 min

Pumpkin Dark Chocolate Fudge

Ingredients:

- Pumpkin puree, 1 cup
- Cashews, soaked overnight, 1 cup
- Dates, ½ cup
- 1 pinch of salt
- Raw honey, ¼ cup
- Cinnamon powder, 1 teaspoon
- Coconut cream, 1 teaspoon
- Cocoa powder, ¼ cup

90

- Coconut oil, ¼ cup
- Vanilla extract, 1 teaspoon

Directions:
1. Pulse all the ingredients in mixer; process until creamy.
2. Add mixture onto plastic with in baking dish; refrigerate for 120 minutes and serve cubes.

Servings: 2
Preparation time: 15 min
Cooking time: 2 h

Avocado Key Lime Pie

Ingredients
For Crust:
- Almonds, 1 cup
- Walnuts, 1 cup
- Dates, 1 cup, pitted
- Lemon juice, 2 tablespoons
- Raw honey, 2 tablespoons
- Coconut oil, 2 tablespoons
- 1 pinch of salt

For Filling:
- Ripe avocados, peeled, 2
- Key limes, juiced, 4
- Lemon zest
- Cashews nuts, soaked overnight, 2 cups
- Raw honey, ½ cup

- 1 pinch salt
- Vanilla extract, 1 teaspoon

Directions:
1. Combine coconut oil, salt, raw honey, lemon juice, almonds, walnuts, lemon as well as dates together to mixer and pulse until creamy. Add it to pie tin and keep it aside.
2. Now add cashews as well as avocados to food processor and process until smooth.
3. Put in zest, lime juice, vanilla, salt as well as raw honey and decant into crust.
4. Refrigerate for an hour before you serve.

Servings: 4
Preparation time: 20 min
Cooking time: 1 h

Apple Cobbler

Ingredients
For Crust:
- Apples, peeled and diced, 2 pounds
- Lemon, juiced, 1
- Lemon zest, 2 tablespoons
- Raw honey, ¼ cup

For Topping:
- Almonds, 1 cup
- Walnuts, 1 cup
- Coconut oil, 2 tablespoons

- Vanilla extract, 2 tablespoons
- Raw honey, 2 tablespoons
- 1 pinch salt

Directions:
1. Marinade raw honey, lemon zest, juice as well as apples together in a shallow bowl. Set aside.
2. Pulse raw honey, salt, vanilla extract, coconut oil, walnuts as well as almonds in food processor until topping is ready. Scatter on apples and serve.

Servings: 6
Preparation time: 5 min
Cooking time: 15 min

Chocolate Covered Figs

Ingredients:
- Dark chocolate chips, 1 cup
- Walnuts halves, 8
- Figs, 8

Directions:
1. Add chocolate chip to the pan and melt.
2. Fill walnuts inside figs and dredge in melted chocolate chips.
3. Bake the mixture for a while and let it stand for 15 minutes on room temperature before serving.

Servings: 4
Preparation time: 5 min
Cooking time: 20 min

Chia Raspberry Pudding

Ingredients:
- Fresh raspberries, 2 cups
- Raw honey, 2 tablespoons
- Chia seeds, ¼ cup
- Lemon juice, 1 teaspoon

Directions:
1. Pulse raspberries, raw honey as well as lemon juice all together in a mixer and set aside by putting it in chia seeds.
2. Let it cool on room temperature for a while before serving.

Servings: 2
Preparation time: 10 min
Cooking time: 15 min

Avocado Chocolate Mousse

Ingredients:
- Ripe avocados, peeled, 2
- Raw cocoa powder, ¼ cup
- Coconut cream, 1 cup
- Raw honey, ¼ cup
- 1 pinch of salt
- Vanilla extract, 1 teaspoon

Directions:
1. Pulse all ingredients in food processor; process until creamy.
2. Chill for 120 minutes before you serve in bowls.

Servings: 2
Preparation time: 10 min
Cooking time: 2 h

Blueberry Mini Pies

Ingredients
For Crust:
- Dates, pitted, 1 cup
- Coconut, shredded, 1 ½ cups
- Almond flour, 1 cup
- Raw honey, 2 tablespoons
- 1 pinch salt

For Filling:
- Almond butter, ½ cup
- Ground almonds, 1 cup
- Blueberries, 3 cups
- Coconut oil, ½ cup
- 1 pinch salt
- Raw honey, ¼ cup
- Lemon juice, 2 tablespoons
- Lemon zest, 1 tablespoon

Directions:
1. Process honey, salt, almond flour, dates as well as shredded coconut in mixer; process until smooth. Press mixture in a pie tin and keep it aside.
2. Add blueberries, butter, almonds, coconut oil, salt, honey, lemon zest as well as lemon juice to blender; process well for filling.

3. Decant filling onto crust, refrigerate for an hour and chop before serving.

Servings: 4
Preparation time: 20 min
Cooking time: 1 h

Strawberry Tart

Ingredients

For Crust:
- Almonds, 2 cups
- Cashews, soaked overnight, ½ cup
- Raw honey, 2 tablespoons
- 1 pinch salt
- Vanilla extract, 1 teaspoon
- Dates, pitted, ½ cup

For Filling:
- Fresh strawberries, halved, 4 cups

Directions:
1. Pulse all ingredients except strawberries in a mixer; process until creamy.
2. Press mixture in a pan; chill for an hour and serve with topped strawberries.

Servings: 4
Preparation time: 10 min
Cooking time: 1 h 15 min

Chocolate Pecan Pie

Ingredients

For Crust:

- Raw almonds, ½ cup
- Pecans, 1 cup
- Dates, pitted, 1 cup
- 1 pinch of salt,
- 1 pinch nutmeg
- Vanilla extract, 1 teaspoon

For Filling:

- Ripe avocado, peeled, 2
- Lemon juice, 2 tablespoons
- Cashews, soaked overnight, ½ cup
- Coconut milk, ½ cup
- Dates, pitted, ½ cup
- Raw honey, ¼ cup
- Raw cocoa powder, ¼ cup
- 1 pinch salt

Directions:

1. Pulse all crust ingredients in food processor; process until smooth and set aside in pie tin.
2. Blend raw honey, salt, cocoa powder, dates, coconut milk, cashews, avocados as well as lemon juice in a mixer to make filling.
3. Decant onto crust and chill for an hour before you serve.

Servings: 4
Preparation time: 15 min
Cooking time: 1 h

Cashew And Date Pudding

Ingredients:

- Dates, pitted, 1 cup
- Cashews, soaked overnight, 1 cup
- Water, ¼ cup
- Raw honey, ¼ cup
- 1 pinch nutmeg
- Cinnamon powder, ½ teaspoon
- Raw cocoa powder, 2 tablespoons
- 1 pinch of salt

Directions:

Pulse all ingredients in food processor; blend until creamy and serve in shallow bowl.

Servings: 2
Preparation time: 5 min
Cooking time: 10 min

Cinnamon Fruit Pancakes

Ingredients:

- Ripe mashed bananas, 2
- Ground flax seeds, 2 cups
- Raw honey, 2 tablespoons
- Cinnamon powder, ½ teaspoon
- Ground ginger, ½ teaspoon
- 1 pinch of salt
- Fresh strawberries, 2 cups

Directions:

1. Mix cinnamon, ginger, salt, flax seeds, bananas as well as raw honey together in a shallow bowl.
2. Scatter mixture onto baking sheet in the form of circles.
3. Keep it in dry as well as warm place for few hours and then serve with fresh, topped strawberries.

Servings: 2
Preparation time: 20 min
Cooking time: 2-3 h

Banana Frozen Treats

Ingredients:

- Large bananas, cut into half, 2
- Dark chocolate, 5 ounces
- Chopped walnuts, ½ cup

Directions:

1. Skew bananas and refrigerate for 120 minutes.
2. Dredge in melted chocolate and serve with garnished walnuts.

Servings: 2
Preparation time: 15 min
Cooking time: 2 h

Strawberry Chocolate Popsicles

Ingredients:

- Strawberries, 2 cups
- Ripe bananas, 2
- Coconut milk, 2 cups
- Cashew nuts, soaked overnight, ½ cup
- Cocoa powder, ¼ cup
- Vanilla extract, 1 teaspoon
- 1 pinch salt
- Raw honey, ¼ cup

Directions:

1. Pulse all ingredients in food processor; process well and transfer to popsicle molds.
2. Refrigerate for 120 minutes.
3. Separate from popsicles and serve.

Servings: 6
Preparation time: 5 min
Cooking time: 15 min

Spicy Dark Chocolate Truffles

Ingredients:

- Vanilla extract, 1 teaspoon
- 1 pinch chili flakes
- Coconut cream, ½ cup
- Raw honey, ¼ cup
- Raw cocoa powder, 1 cup

- Coconut oil, melted, 1 cup
- Cocoa powder for rolling, ¼ cup

Directions:
1. Pulse all ingredients in food processor and chill for 25 minutes.
2. Make balls of the mixture and roll through powder before you serve.

Servings: 4
Preparation time: 30 min
Cooking time: 10 min

Banana And Coconut Bars

Ingredients
For Crust:
- Shredded coconut, ½ cup
- Cashews, soaked overnight, 1 cup
- Dates, pitted, 1 cup
- Coconut milk, ¼ cup
- 1 pinch nutmeg

For Filling:
- Ripe bananas, 2
- Almond butter, ½ cup
- Coconut milk, ¼ cup
- Raw honey, 4 tablespoons
- Coconut flakes, 1 cup
- Coconut oil, ¼ cup
- Vanilla extract, 1 teaspoon

Directions:

1. Pulse nutmeg, coconut milk, dates, shredded coconut as well as cashews in food processor; blend until creamy.
2. Scatter mixture onto plastic lying on baking sheet and keep it aside.
3. Blend coconut oil, vanilla extract, coconut flakes, coconut milk, raw honey, bananas as well as almond butter to make filling.
4. Spread mixture onto crust; refrigerate for 120 minutes and chop before serving.

Servings: 6
Preparation time: 20 min
Cooking time: 2 h

Made in the USA
Middletown, DE
19 March 2018